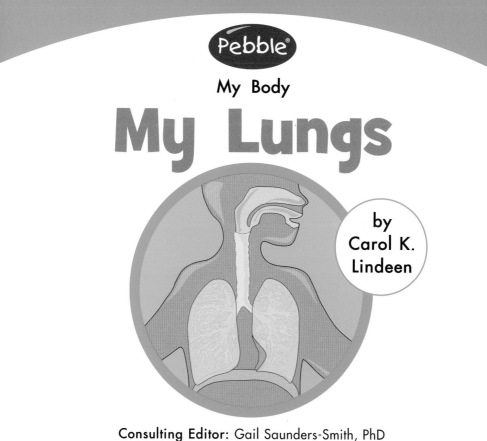

Pebble®

My Body

My Lungs

by
Carol K.
Lindeen

Consulting Editor: Gail Saunders-Smith, PhD

Consultant: James R. Hubbard, MD
Fellow in the American Academy of Pediatrics
Iowa Medical Society, West Des Moines, Iowa

Capstone
press®

Mankato, Minnesota

Pebble Books are published by Capstone Press,
151 Good Counsel Drive, P.O. Box 669, Mankato, Minnesota 56002.
www.capstonepress.com

1 2 3 4 5 6 12 11 10 09 08 07

Library of Congress Cataloging-in-Publication Data
Lindeen, Carol, 1976–
     My lungs / by Carol K. Lindeen.
     p. cm.—(Pebble Books. My body)
     Summary: "Simple text and photographs describe human lungs and their
function"—Provided by publisher.
     Includes bibliographical references and index.
     ISBN-13: 978-0-7368-6692-7 (hardcover)
     ISBN-10: 0-7368-6692-2 (hardcover)
     ISBN-13: 978-0-7368-7836-4 (softcover pbk.)
     ISBN-10: 0-7368-7836-X (softcover pbk.)
1. Lungs—Juvenile literature. 2. Respiration—Juvenile literature. I. Title. II. Series.
QP121.L56 2007
612.2—dc22   2006013829

Note to Parents and Teachers

The My Body set supports national science standards related to
anatomy and the basic structure and function of the human body.
This book describes and illustrates the lungs. The photographs
support early readers in understanding the text. The repetition
of words and phrases helps early readers learn new words. This
book also introduces early readers to subject-specific vocabulary
words, which are defined in the Glossary section. Early readers
may need assistance to read some words and to use the Table of
Contents, Glossary, Read More, Internet Sites, and Index sections
of the book.

Table of Contents

Breathing

I breathe in and out.
My lungs help me
blow out birthday candles.

My lungs help me
blow bubbles.
My lungs help me
sing and run.

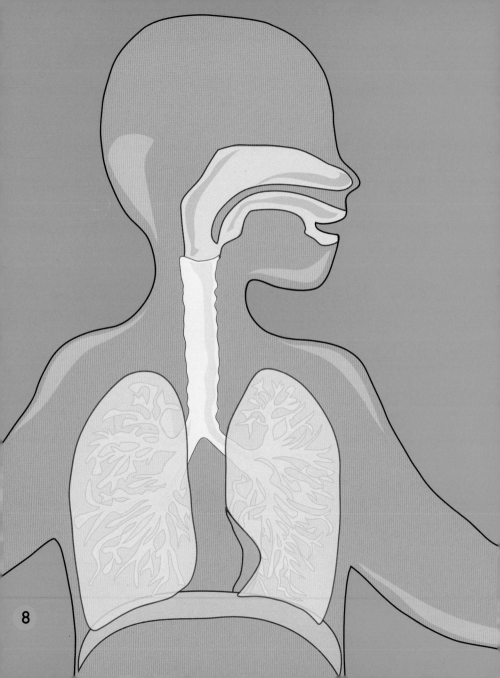

8

On the Inside

I have two lungs
inside my chest.
My right lung is
a little bigger.

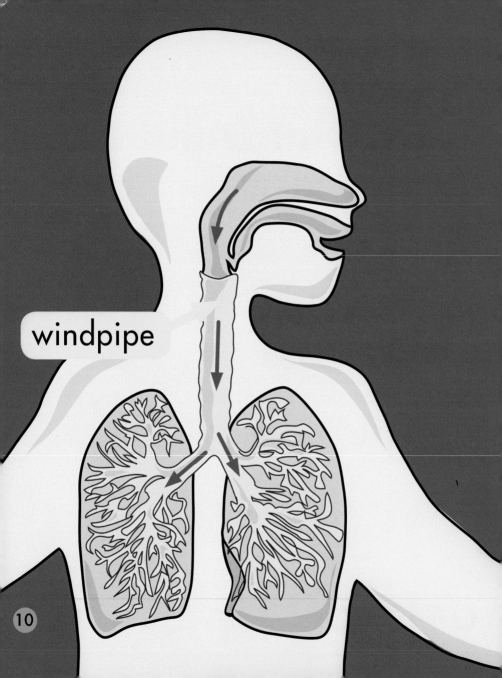

windpipe

When I breathe in,
air goes down
my windpipe
and into my lungs.

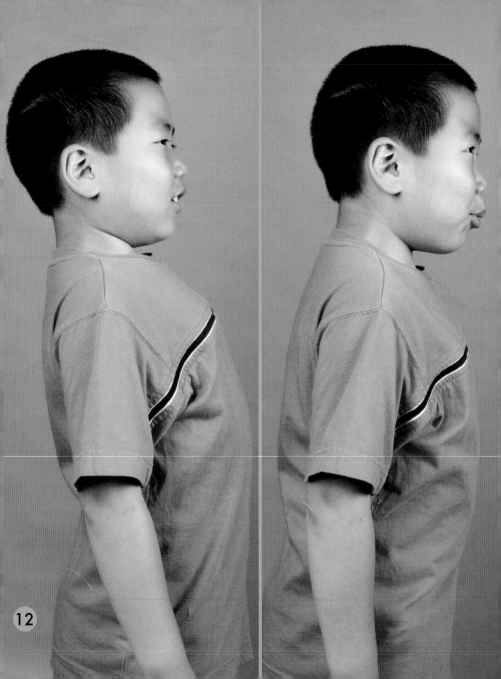

My lungs fill with air
when I inhale.
Air has oxygen
that I need to live.

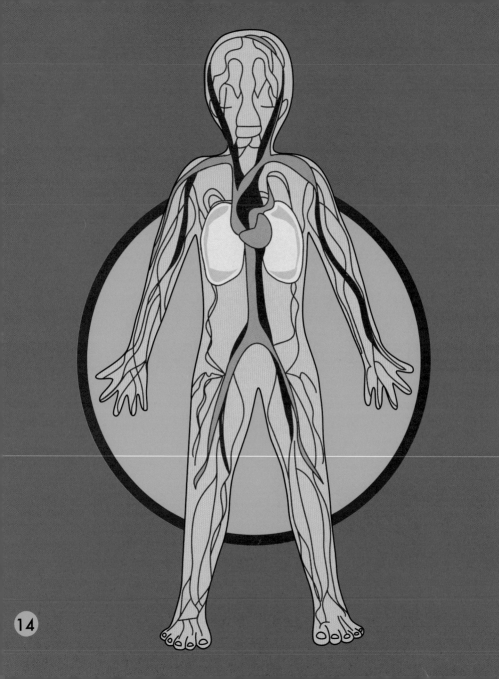

My Lungs and My Body

My lungs send oxygen
to my blood.
Then my heart pumps
blood and oxygen
through my body.

I breathe out
carbon dioxide.
My body does not need
carbon dioxide.

I breathe faster
when I am active.
Being active
helps my lungs
stay healthy and strong.

I breathe more slowly
when I sleep.
My lungs work hard
all day and all night.

Glossary

active—busy playing and exercising

blood—the liquid that your heart pumps through your body

breathe—to take air in and out of the lungs

carbon dioxide—a gas that people breathe out

inhale—to breathe in

lung—a large body part inside the chest; the left lung is a little smaller than the right lung so it can make space for the heart.

oxygen—a gas found in the air; people and animals need oxygen to live.

windpipe—a tube that connects the mouth and nose to the lungs; air goes in and out of the body through the windpipe; the windpipe is also called the trachea.

Read More

Ballard, Carol. *Lungs.* Body Focus. Chicago: Heinemann, 2003.

Rau, Dana Meachen. *My Lungs.* What's Inside Me? Tarrytown, N.Y.: Benchmark Books, 2005.

Internet Sites

FactHound offers a safe, fun way to find Internet sites related to this book. All of the sites on FactHound have been researched by our staff.

Here's how:

1. Visit *www.facthound.com*
2. Choose your grade level.
3. Type in this book ID **0736866922** for age-appropriate sites. You may also browse subjects by clicking on letters, or by clicking on pictures and words.
4. Click on the **Fetch It** button.

FactHound will fetch the best sites for you!

Index

Word Count: 130
Grade: 1
Early-Intervention Level: 14

Editorial Credits
Mari Schuh, editor; Bobbi J. Wyss, designer; Sandy D'Antonio, illustrator;
   Wanda Winch, photo researcher; Kelly Garvin, photo stylist

Photo Credits
Capstone Press/Karon Dubke, all